Witold Lutosławski

His life *&* work *with authoritative* text *and* selected music

T0061479

WISE PUBLICATIONS
London / New York / Paris / Sydney / Copenhagen / Berlin / Madrid / Hong Kong / Tokyo

Witold Lutosławski

a short biography

WITOLD LUTOSLAWSKI's life and music (born in 1913, he died aged 81 in 1994) pivoted around the turbulent events of Poland's twentieth century. When he was just five, his family fled eastwards to Moscow to escape the incoming troop lines of World War I, only for his politically active father to be executed by the Bolsheviks; while serving in the Polish forces during World War II, Lutoslawski was captured by the *Wehrmacht* (he then made a daring escape); his brother was captured by Soviet troops and died in a Siberian labour camp; Stalinism, Polish Communism and the Cold War brought further deprivations. One might therefore imagine that Lutoslawski's music would be filled with images of violence, trauma and lament. So it is. Yet his style is rarely pessimistic and cynical, and never relentlessly tragic. Like his career and life as a whole, his pieces often tell a story of tragedy transcended. Within the meticulously crafted worlds of his scores — by turns viscerally dramatic, witty and ironic, delicately beautiful and savagely expressive — he sought to escape from daily life and into a personal realm of the imagination, in order to search for forms of perfection absent in the wider world. Lutoslawski thereby created works that paid powerful testimony to his life experiences, while transcending the circumstances of their creation to address greater concerns.

Lutoslawski's musical output unfolded over three broad stylistic phases. Each phase began with a period during which Lutoslawski mastered crucial aspects of his compositional language, followed by a period of mastery when he produced the series of *chefs-d'oeuvre* for which he would become, and remain, internationally renowned as the towering figure of Polish twentieth-century music. His emergence onto the world stage followed Stalin's death in 1953 and Poland's cultural 'thaw' — a brief respite from cultural censure for most artists, but sustained for the country's composers — which permitted musicians to experiment with a range of avant-garde styles. Lutoslawski forged his unique contemporary voice in this 'middle' period by exploring tensions between the classicist sensibilities that had underpinned his 'early' period's neoclassical compositions (a style that had already brought him to a position of preeminence in Poland, not least through his extraordinary Concerto for Orchestra of 1950–54) and more radical alternatives. As such, while he pioneered individual solutions to post-tonal problems of pitch, rhythm, form, texture and instrumentation, he did so as part of a productive dialogue between high modernism and earlier wellsprings of musical expressivity ranging from Haydn, Beethoven and Chopin to Debussy, Prokofiev, Ravel and Stravinsky. The fruits of that exchange can be heard in 'middle' period masterpieces including his *Livre pour Orchestre* (1968), Cello Concerto (1969–70), *Les Espaces du Sommeil* (1975) and *Mi-parti* (1975–6), and 'late' period triumphs such as *Chain 3* (1986), his Piano Concerto (1987–8) and Symphony No.4 (1988–92).

Like Poland's two other indisputably great art music composers, Chopin and Szymanowski, Lutoslawski was also a virtuoso pianist — his graduation from Warsaw's music conservatory in 1936 was marked, in part, by performances of Beethoven's Piano Concerto No.4 in G major, Op.58 and Chopin's Ballade No. 4 in F minor, Op.52; shortly before this, Lutoslawski had completed a fascinating Piano Sonata (1934) of his own as a vehicle for his precocious emerging talents. Regretfully, however, unlike his illustrious predecessors, the piano faded as a focus of his compositional endeavours. Lutoslawski instead developed his mastery of the symphony orchestra — his true instrument. Nevertheless, alongside its role in significant works such as the *Partita* for solo violin and piano (1984), and its near constant presence within Lutoslawski's orchestral forces, there are numerous gems for solo piano dotted throughout his career, culminating in his Piano Concerto. Many of those gems are gathered in this album, which offers snapshots of his idiomatic writing for the instrument, and glimpses of the enduring compositional concerns that interconnect so many of his pieces.

Nicholas Reyland
February 2014

Published by
WISE PUBLICATIONS
14-15 Berners Street, London W1T 3LJ, UK.

Exclusive Distributors:

MUSIC SALES LIMITED
Distribution Centre, Newmarket Road,
Bury St Edmunds, Suffolk IP33 3YB, UK.

MUSIC SALES CORPORATION
180 Madison Avenue, 24th Floor,
New York NY 10016, USA.

MUSIC SALES PTY LIMITED
Units 3-4, 17 Willfox Street, Condell Park,
NSW 2200, Australia.

Order No. AM1008513
ISBN: 978-1-78305-465-7
This book © Copyright 2014 Wise Publications,
a division of Music Sales Limited.

Edited by Sam Lung.
Biography and introductory texts by Nicholas Reyland.
Music engraved and processed by Camden Music Services,
Elius Gravure Musicale and Sam Lung.
Cover design by Chloe Alexander.
Photo page 28 Grzegorz Roginski/Forum.

Printed in the EU.

Folk Melodies

THE devastation of cities such as Warsaw during World War II was paralleled by the Nazi occupation's impact on Poland's musical life and institutions. Post-war musical reconstruction thus took many forms, with musicians rebuilding orchestras, publishing houses and — in the case of works including Lutoslawski's *Folk Melodies* (1945) — creating educational resources and a renewed connection to the country's musical heritage. 'I wanted', the composer wrote, 'to make the rich melodies of Polish folklore accessible to the youngest performers'. Such tasks also offered the composer an important means of making ends meet in straightened times, in this case by fulfilling a commission from the newly founded state-owned publishing house, Polskie Wydawnictwo Muzyczne (PWM).

Drawing together twelve folk melodies from a collection by Jerzy Olszewski, Lutoslawski elaborated each tune according to the following general method: the melody, presented in its original diatonic form, is accompanied by a second melodic line or chords of a mostly non-diatonic nature: convention thereby mixes with modernity. An obvious model is Bartók's *Microkosmos*, but the counterpointing of tonal materials with chromatic accompaniments also links the *Folk Melodies* to Lutoslawski's more adventurous earlier works. The results are idiosyncratic and charming.

'There Is A Path, There Is' and 'The Shepherd Girl' originated from the Podlasie region to the east of Warsaw; 'An Apple Hangs On The Apple-tree' comes from Sieradz; according to Charles Bodman Rae's fine introduction to Lutoslawski's life and music, 1994's *The Music of Lutoslawski*, the title of 'Master Michael' relates to the composer's own early childhood in Drozdowo (it is a waltz from the Kurpie region); 'The Grove', 'The Gander' and 'The Schoolmaster' are all Silesian dances.

Rae identifies one constant of Lutoslawski's musical styles across his career in the voicing of the *Folk Melodies*: a tune at the top, a chromatic accompaniment, and a resonant open sonority, such as a perfect fifth, in the bass (as at the *Allegro moderato* in 'Master Michael'). Another trait one might note occurs when the bass drops out and a melody slips free of its tonal anchor on a sea of chromatic substitutions — the manner in which the musical path is lost, for instance, in 'There Is A Path, There Is'. And often, Lutoslawski forgoes a sense of simple closure for something more poised, as at the end of 'The Gander'; the plain A major triad at the end of 'Master Michael' sounds similarly uncanny. The pianist, however, should not turn such moments into heavy musical weather. They are modest examples, in these unpretentious but endearing pieces, of Lutoslawski's ability to shape expressivity through compositional methods every bit as characterful as the sources of his *Folk Melodies*.

Folk Melodies

III. There Is A Path, There Is

Witold Lutosławski

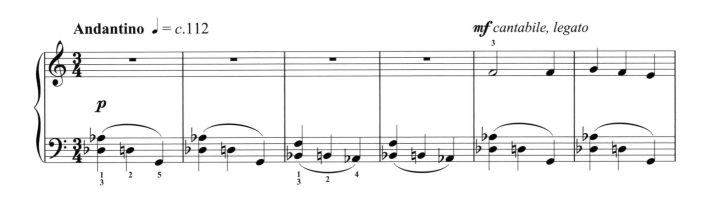

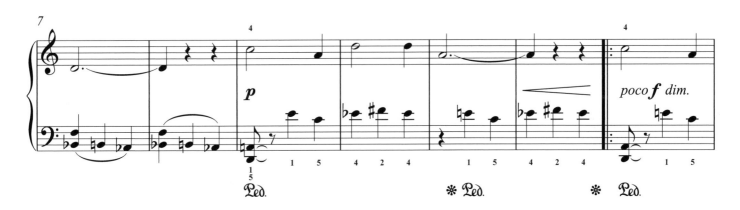

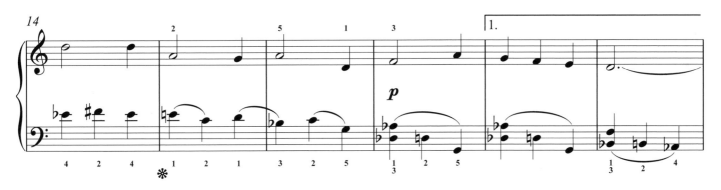

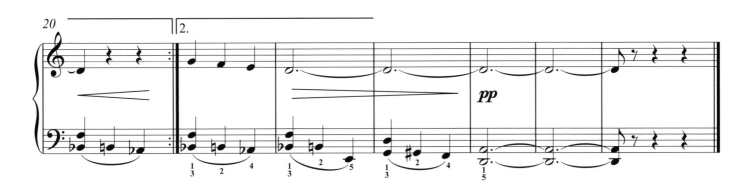

Folk Melodies
IV. The Shepherd Girl

Witold Lutosławski

Folk Melodies

V. An Apple Hangs On The Apple-tree

Witold Lutosławski

Folk Melodies

VII. Master Michael

Witold Lutosławski

Folk Melodies

XI. The Gander

Witold Lutosławski

Folk Melodies

X. The Grove

Witold Lutosławski

Folk Melodies

XII. The Schoolmaster

Witold Lutosławski

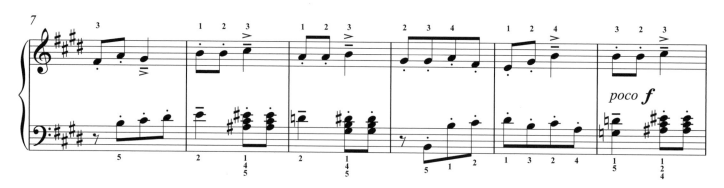

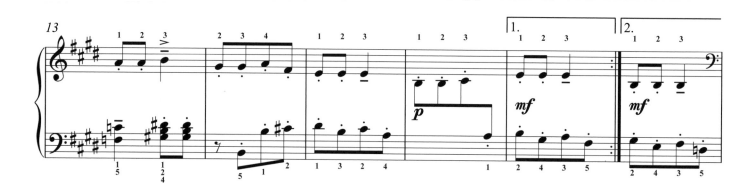

Bucolics

I. Allegro vivace *and* V. Allegro marciale

LUTOSLAWSKI'S own description of his *Bucolics* (1952) — as miniatures that developed the model of his *Folk Melodies* (1945, see below) and which were similarly written with young pianists in mind — belies the fact that their freer transformations of folk material, sophistication and inventiveness shaped a set deserving of being deemed 'the best of the works leading to the Concerto for Orchestra' by no less an expert than Steven Stucky (writing in his pioneering 1981 study *Lutoslawski and His Music*). They also encapsulate the gist of Lutoslawski's neoclassical style, but, more importantly, the *Bucolics* demonstrate the manner in which, throughout his career, he mobilized technique to personal expressive ends. These include a desire to play with listener expectations — intensely dramatic in some of the later pieces, more Puckish here — marking one of the constants of his music. Trickier to play, then, than the *Folk Melodies* (Lutoslawski himself gave their première in 1953), Stucky nonetheless suggests that they are 'still quite possible for students of intermediate accomplishments'. They are certainly worth the effort.

Each of the five movements is based on folk tunes from the heavily forested Polish region of Kurpie. Lutoslawski adopted them from a collection by a priest, Father Wladyslaw Skierkowski — one of the many Polish musicians to be lost in the Nazi concentration camps. Yet Lutoslawski does not simply set the melodies. Rather, he uses the tunes as motivic resources for his own thematic inventiveness, in a manner he would soon perfect in the Concerto for Orchestra. The opening and closing *Allegro marciale* movements are a joy.

The first's ABA form contrasts bright diatonic tonality with (from bars 29-45) a subdued bitonal development; the restoration of the former realm then leads to a codetta bridging both sound-worlds. It is Lutoslawski's control of rhythm and meter, though, that is a particular delight: the initial shift from 3/4 to 2/4 sends one sliding onto the slippery ice of those semiquaver runs in the left hand — and it takes a while to recover one's bearings. Throughout the piece, Lutoslawski plays with our metrical expectations, making its journey from stability to instability and back a game of both harmony and rhythm.

The final *Allegro marciale* is even more cunning: its opening bar of 5/4, suggesting a tonal centre of F sharp, would be misleading enough, followed as it is by a sprightly 2/4 theme in D. Yet Lutoslawski allows an extra beat of the F sharp drone to creep into the first bar of the theme, undermining its new meter and its harmony. The ensuing music dances around and about these slippery, exuberant ideas.

Bucolics

I. Allegro vivace

Witold Lutosławski

Bucolics

V. Allegro marciale

Witold Lutosławski

Invention

AFTER 1953's *Three Pieces For The Young* (see p.29), Lutoslawski wrote only one more composition for solo piano: his *Invention* of 1968. This short *pièce d'occasion* was dedicated to Stefan Sledzinski on his 71st birthday. A Polish musicologist, Sledzinski had been a Professor at the prewar Warsaw Conservatory where Lutoslawski had trained as a pianist and composer. As the recipient of such a gift, Sledzinski was in fine company: Lutoslawski tributes are few and far between, but include presents for musicians including Elliott Carter (*Slides*, 1988) and Anne-Sophie Mutter (a *Lullaby* for violin and piano, 1989, written to mark the birth of her child).

This miniature, composed on the cusp of the period of modernist mastery beginning with *Livre pour Orchestre* the same year, offers a snapshot of another one of Lutoslawski's stylistic constants. The constant, already audible in his *Two Studies* of 1940–41 (see p.38), is Lutoslawski's fascination with creating post-tonal harmonic contrasts through a simple but powerful alternative to diatonic modes and keys: melodies and harmonies constructed from a limited range of types of interval. In the first bar of the *Interlude*, for example, the piano outlines (reading upwards from bass to treble) the pitches B, C, E, F, A — a sonority built of interlocking semitones and major thirds. In bars 2–4, a new pitch range unfolds — C♯, D♯, E, F♯, G — from semitones and whole tones. For Lutoslawski, the contrast between such constructions, each with its own harmonic colour or (in his preferred word) quality, was comparable in terms of both audibility and expressive nuance to the contrast between major to minor in the tonal system. Many of his pieces are built around such oppositions — as here, where the two-part inventiveness (note the shades of Bach in the counterpoint between the left- and right-hand lines) comes from a search for rapprochement between the two intervallic qualities, but also between their lyrical and introspective characters.

Invention

Witold Lutosławski

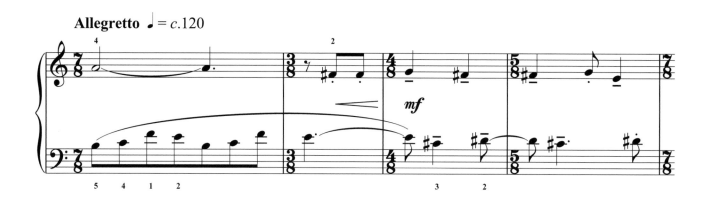

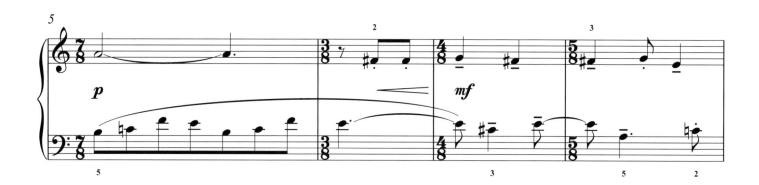

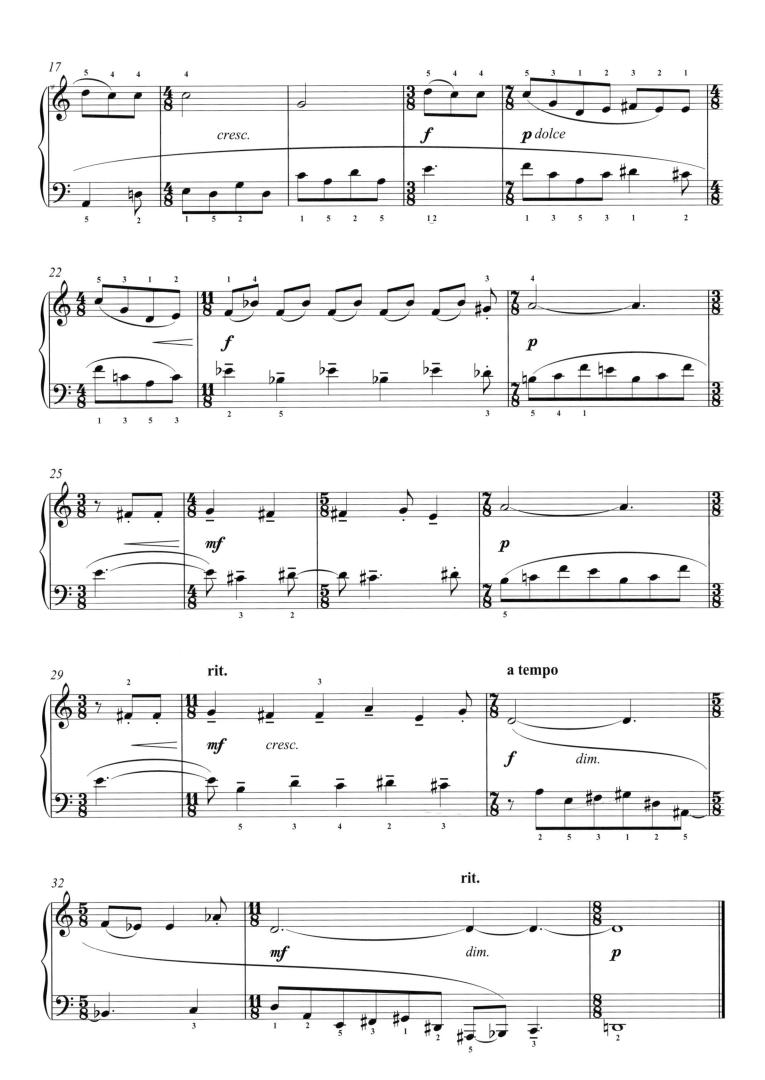

Concerto for Piano and Orchestra

3rd movement

PASSAGES in Lutoslawski's *Concerto for Piano and Orchestra* match the quality of the other peaks of his late period, including his magnificent final major composition, Symphony No.4, begun in the year the piano concerto was completed for Krystian Zimerman, who gave its premiere at the 1988 Salzburg Festival. The third movement of the Concerto's four-part scheme, the start and end of which are composed for piano alone and joined together in this collection, also make one regretful that Lutoslawski so rarely returned to piano writing after the 1950s. Lutoslawski spoke of 'catching up with arrears' in the 1980s — returning to projects he had abandoned in his youth, such as concertos for piano and violin. Perhaps unsurprisingly, therefore, his piano concerto contains passages that remind one of his musical pasts. The writing is beautifully idiomatic, in part because it is peppered with allusions to musicians who influenced Lutoslawski's stylistic development, formed the backbone of his repertoire as a pianist in the 1930s–40s, and inspired his approach to writing for the piano: Bartók, Debussy and Ravel, but also Beethoven and Chopin.

The slow third movement is a Chopin nocturne turned dark night of the soul. It was inspired, some have whispered, by Lutoslawski's experience of Martial Law in Poland in the mid 1980s, when the U.S.S.R.-backed regime was cracking down on the Solidarity trade union and what would prove, ultimately, to be an unstoppable momentum towards democracy and freedom from Soviet control. Such freedoms were by no means assured, however, in the period when Lutoslawski was composing this work, and it is not difficult to imagine why some believe the tensions of the time are reflected in the music. Its Largo, for instance, is one of the most sustained and searching passages of lyricism in all Lutoslawski, and initiates the movement's contrasting of calmer, more reflective material with gestures of ebullient liberty.

A note to performers: accidentals here, i.e. sharps and flats, only refer to the pitch they immediately precede in a bar. The pedalling is carefully defined in the score, and particular care should be taken to observe this.

Concerto for Piano and Orchestra

3rd movement (excerpts)

Witold Lutosławski

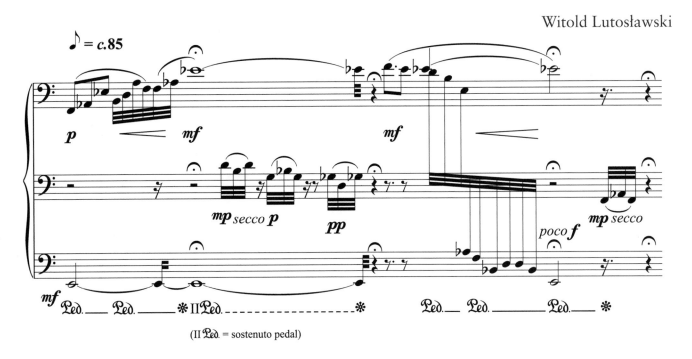

(II 🎵 = sostenuto pedal)

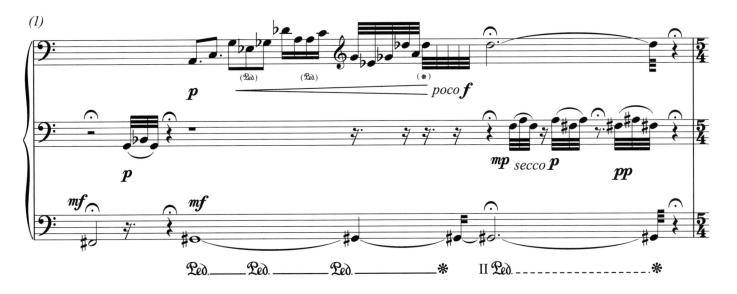

Three Pieces For The Young

A FURTHER postwar commission from PWM to provide piano music for players in the early stages of their studies gave Lutoslawski the opportunity to compose his *Three Pieces For The Young* in 1953. He received this invitation while hard at work on what would become his first masterpiece — the Concerto for Orchestra — and this may explain why, in writing this trio of studies, Lutoslawski steered clear of folk tunes and adopted a different voice to his earlier *Bucolics* and *Folk Melodies*. These pieces sound a little more rigorous, especially in terms of their more straightforward rhythms, as befits their intended nature as exercises (the first is a four-finger exercise, the second explores interlocking chordal patterns, and the third repeated chords). However, stepping free of folk music also permitted Lutoslawski to explore alternative compositional concerns — and to nod to another composer.

The first of the *Three Pieces For The Young*, an *Allegro*, is fiendish fun. Its G major tonal centre is there from the start, but only feels secure in the off-hand brilliance of its final bar. Before this, one is kept guessing by the harmonic patterns giving momentum to the rapid semiquaver movement: interlocking minor and major thirds, in the right hand, and a chromatically expanding and contracting pattern in the left. Both are sounds one hears again in Lutoslawski's later stylistic phases. The second piece, 'An Air', is emotionally more substantial. The undulating major and minor triads — which would soon be heard again in the *Dance Preludes* (1954), and then somewhat later, draped in a glimmering veil of quartertones, at the start of *Livre pour Orchestre* — explore a plangent expressive ambiguity. Also typically, although the music reaches a forceful climax — the *forte* in bar 26, where the undulating patterns are powerfully performed between the hands — there is no sense of easy resolution. The air is cleared, instead, by the closing 'March', one of several Lutoslawski movements — such as the finale of the Double Concerto (1979–80) — to evoke Prokofiev in its deft satirizing of the kind of strident march to which citizens of the Soviet Bloc would became somewhat overexposed.

Three Pieces For The Young

I. Four-Finger Exercise

Witold Lutosławski

Three Pieces For The Young

II. An Air

Witold Lutosławski

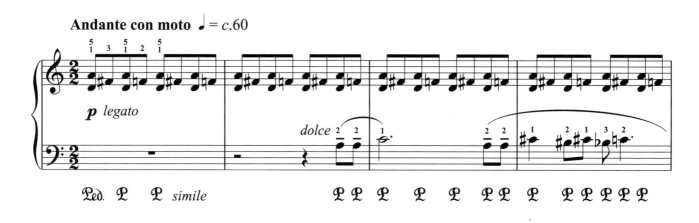

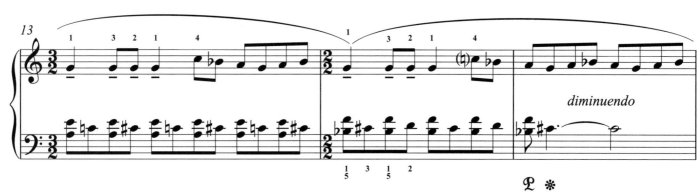

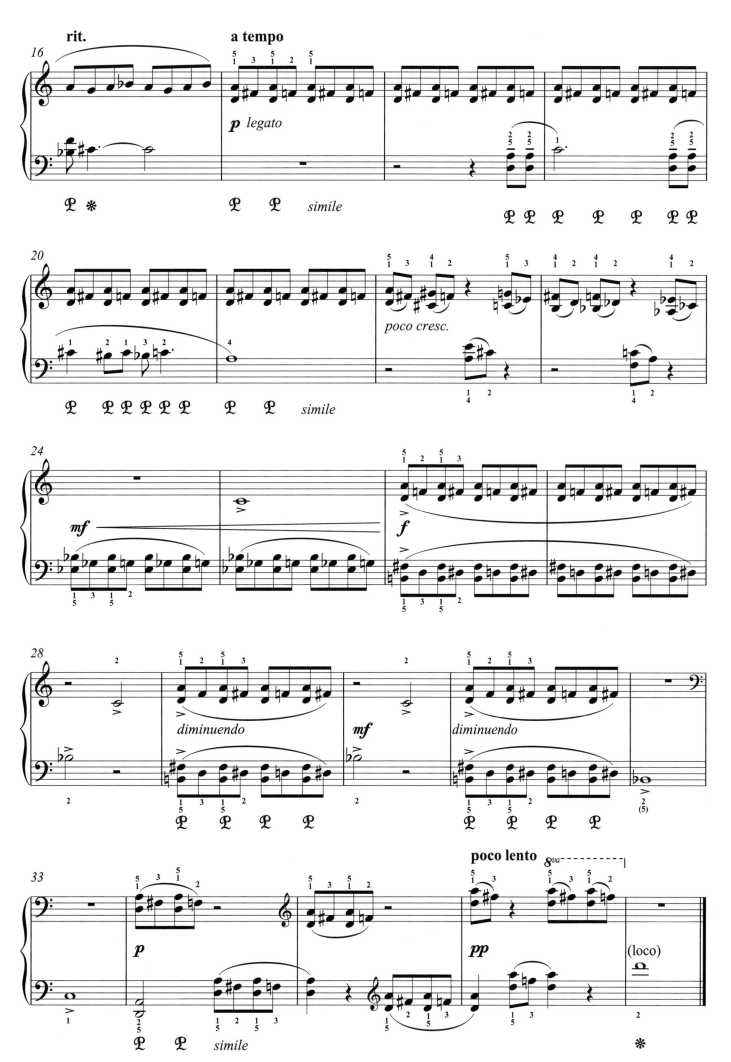

Three Pieces For The Young
III. March

poco meno mosso   Tempo I

Prelude

from Strawchain

WHILE the fact that Lutoslawski continued to compose children's songs and pieces inspired by folk music well into the 1950s suggests a degree of continuity between the *Folk Melodies* of 1945 and *Strawchain* (1950–51), the symbolism of working with such materials in Poland had changed significantly in the interim. The motivations that had led to Lutoslawski's folk-inspired and educational pieces of the immediate post-war period — a sense of civic duty mixed with lightly worn pride in Poland's musical heritage — remained constant, but was now set against a backdrop of Stalinist requirements that Polish composers shackle pieces inspired by their country's folk music to the formulae of Soviet socialist realism. One intention for such art works — 'socialist in content, national in form' went the slogan — was to give barefaced propaganda a disarmingly familiar mask. A darker motivation was the desire to condition the minds of Poles to endorse the ideals and goals of Soviet Communism. This proved tricky: converting Poland to communism, Stalin allegedly remarked, was a bit like trying to saddle a cow. Lutoslawski was a composer of the bovine ilk.

While he did pen a handful of mass song commissions — anthem-like popular songs with political texts or subtexts — for the most part Lutoslawski succeeded in sidestepping more ideologically onerous work during Poland's dark decade. He achieved this, in part, through the sheer scale of his musical ability by the early 1950s: his first period of mastery (the peak of his neoclassical phase) coincided with the imposition of socialist realism. His inventiveness, technique and vision — as heard in pieces like the *Silesian Triptych* (1951), Concerto for Orchestra and *Dance Preludes* — enabled him to get away with audacities of a kind that led to strictures for lesser figures, while paying little more than lip service to the Party's aesthetic demands. For the most part, however, Lutoslawski steered clear of politics and made his daily bread by taking regular commissions to write music for the young or light radio. The actual 'Chain of straw' is the song — a theme and variations — that forms the last of the eight pieces in the published collection prefaced by this Stravinskian prelude. Scored originally for wind quintet, the 'Prelude' has a simple ABAB form, piquant contrasts between its by turns perky and rustic themes, and an impudent codetta.

Prelude
from Strawchain

Witold Lutosławski

Two Studies

I. Allegro

FTER escaping from the *Wehrmacht* and fleeing home to Warsaw, Lutoslawski's pianistic abilities became his primary means of supporting his family during the Nazi occupation of the Polish capital. Warsaw developed a sort of ersatz café society during World War II: a mirage of civilised practice and cultural continuity in the midst of increasingly horrific realities. The mirage also offered paid work for gifted pianists.

The Nazis had banned performances of Chopin as expressions of nationalistic sentiment. Allusions to Chopin were much trickier to police, especially in music that would not be aired publicly until after the war. Lutoslawski's first study (1940–41) — a workout for pianist and composer alike — begins with a nod to Chopin's C major Etude, Op.10, No.1 (the ascending broken chord figure) and was intended to begin a more extended set also modeled on the example of his predecessor. The piece's explosive opening, however, unleashes conflicts typical of Lutoslawski, not Chopin: the stability of the 4/4 meter and pedal Cs is immediately undermined by scrabbling chromaticism, unpredictable metrical shifts and free-flowing contrapuntal invention. These materials are derived from the composer's object of 'study' here: an interest in intervallic pairings (the tones and semitones of the scale figures, and the perfect fourths and fifths that sometimes underpin them) and, as such, sources of harmonic contrast that developed into a hallmark of Lutoslawski's modernist style. Here, the key ideas chase each other through a conventional ternary (ABA) form mapping a journey of departure and return. Expressively, though, one hears nervous, even manic, energy released into flight and unable to find points of repose or much stability — save for brief moments of arrival, such as the pomposo climax that sets the scene for the return of the opening explosion.

Two Studies

I. Allegro

Witold Lutosławski

41

Paganini Variations

(opening)

Witold Lutosławski
(arr. Sam Lung)

F Lutoslawski's first *Study* of 1940–41 sounds like the music of wartime, the most famous composition he completed during World War II, his *Variations on a Theme by Paganini*, is music for the mirage of cultural stability created by Warsaw's makeshift café society during that war. Witty, elegant and touching, the set is the sole surviving fruit of the arrangements Lutoslawski and fellow composer Andrzej Panufnik created to play in their celebrated wartime piano duo. (The score escaped the Nazi razing of Warsaw on the back of a handcart pulled by Lutoslawski, along with a few other prized scores and vital possessions, in 1945.) Based on the transcription of a Paganini performance of variations on his Caprice No.24 for solo violin, Lutoslawski's arrangement also drew on his wartime piano duo's delight in improvisations placing familiar materials in unfamiliar contexts — the tune of a Schubert song, say, to an accompaniment of Ravellian harmony. Hence the kaleidoscopic expressivity of a set of *Variations* that, united by the stylistic hallmarks of Lutoslawski's neoclassical style, still delights audiences today.

The piece begins with a thematic statement that doubles as a statement of compositional intent: Paganini's famous melody, spryly articulated, skips in and out of the harmonic and gestural potholes that dog, but never diminish, the music's essential ebullience.

Allegro capriccioso ($\quad = c.144$)

123456789

Bringing you the words and the music

All the latest music in print... rock & pop plus jazz, blues, country, classical and the best in West End show scores.

- Books to match your favourite CDs.

- Book-and-CD titles with high quality backing tracks for you to play along to. Now you can play guitar or piano with your favourite artist... or simply sing along!

- Audition songbooks with CD backing tracks for both male and female singers for all those with stars in their eyes.

- Can't read music? No problem, you can still play all the hits with our wide range of chord songbooks.

- Check out our range of instrumental tutorial titles, taking you from novice to expert in no time at all!

- Musical show scores include *The Phantom Of The Opera*, *Les Misérables*, *Mamma Mia* and many more hit productions.

- DVD master classes featuring the techniques of top artists.